Atmospherics

Atmospherics
LOHREN GREEN

A CLEARSOUND Book from QUALE PRESS

"Dankness and Cathedrals" and "Shadows" appeared in *32 Poems*.
"Dankness and Cathedrals" also appeared in the anthology,
Old Flame (WordFarm, Seattle, 2012).

Author's Note: I'd like to express my appreciation for the wonderfully unique perspectives of William Pallister and Daniel Coffeen — their friendships flow through this book and through my life. Thanks also to my fishing friends with whom I have explored rivers, discovered seams, and relished time: David Morris, Jon Provisor, Paul Wehner, Eric Freitag, Darin Freitag, and Michael Holt. Some of this book was written during a residency at the Headlands Center for the Arts — my thanks to everyone at the Headlands, along with the play of sun and fog there. Thanks, too, to Leslie Shows who kindly provided a detail from one of her stunning paintings for the cover. My gratitude to Gian Lombardo and Quale Press for the generously energetic interest in, and support of, this work. Finally, my thanks to my love Eva for many, many things.

Copyright © 2014 by Lohren Green

Cover image: Leslie Shows, *Arches*, 2010 (detail).
Copyright © Leslie Shows

ISBN: 978-1-935835-11-0
LCCN: 2014900642

A ClearSound Book from Quale Press
www.quale.com

Table of Contents

Introduction 1

1.0 The Concepts: Constellations and Seams
    Constellations and Seams 5

2.0 The Elements: Airs, Gravities, Times, Minds, Lights, Sounds
    Sample Atmospheres (Table 2.1) 11
  Airs
    Dankness and Cathedrals 15
    Cherry Blossoms 16
    Certain Doings of Dogs and Cats 18
    Perfumed Skin 19
  Gravities
    Equatorial Lift 22
    Momentum 24
  Times
    Antique Clock Shop 28
    Beach Blur 30
    Subway Cycles 31
    Museum Idiosyncrasies 32
    The Beach City Estuary 34
  Minds
    Library Concentrations 39
    Figments of Mind 40
    Food and Dreams 42
    Simpatico and Schooling Fish 43
    Mental Dawnings 44
  Lights
    Iris Light 49
    Shadows 50
    Night and Day (Table 2.2) 53
    Television Light 54
  Sounds
    The *Patio Escondido* and Its Fountains 59
    Sonic City Jumble 60
    Ambient Music 61

3.0 Applications: Studies Prominently Involving Multiple Elements
    Camouflage   65
    The Produce Aisle   66
    Pluralist Symphony   67
    Terroir   68
    Current Trends in Atmospherics   70

For Laszlo and Simone

Introduction

Atmospherics encompasses topics as varied as the flow of time in museums, the play of momentum through a sports event, and the expression of food in dreams. Far from restricting itself to the dynamics of the Earth's gravity-spun gases, ATMOSPHERICS is, quite generally, the study of mooded happening.

To feel what this abstraction means, look up one bright and bustling afternoon and perhaps your eye will happen upon a daytime moon quietly pulling at our Earth. It is somewhat surprising, hung there, distantly incongruous in the pale blue sky, and yet it usually feels somehow welcome. This other side of the night moon's silvery-cool elegance is instead a coy glint of exposure within the vast glare of insolation. The daytime moon is, like everything else, both a physical and a mooded force: it is a specific effusion of lights and pulls and dispositions.

Now see how that daytime moon blends into, for example, a *patio escondido* of southern Spain, into that cool embrace of thick walls about potted plants, broken tiles, and the occasional cigarette butt, where the plunks of a fountain's droplets periodically ripple across the patio and out its wrought iron gate. It is all doubly effusive — the incongruous moonlight, the playing droplets, the arid clays, the unwavering plants. They exude the varied forces that flow together to become this atmospheric bay within old Europe's heavy overhang of blunt summer heat.

The patio's atmosphere is a plurality in perpetual flux. It is a profusion of details, each of which is constantly making sense, and yet it is also somehow a composite that has a sense — a sense that changes in loose concert with everything in and around it. The entirety of this loose concert is our cosmos: the vast, affective bath of everything in everything that at every possible scale, and through each passing instant, is unique. How within this massive, flexing churn does any event feel like anything in particular at all? The hypothesis is poetries.

1 | The Concepts
Constellations and Seams

Constellations and Seams

Atmospheres are infinitely varied, constantly changing, and highly specific And yet they can be explored with the help of just two basic concepts: constellations and seams.

CONSTELLATIONS are groupings of individuals. These groupings might be as diverse as flora or homogeneous as cogs, small as quarks or immense as galaxies, enduring as granite or fleeting as a shiver. Stars can, of course, form constellations, as can the emerald shoots of rice plants in paddies, the stringed instruments of an ensemble, or the attitudes of students and teacher in a classroom

The flowing zones of interaction that emerge between individuals within constellations, and between various constellations, are called seams. A SEAM, then, is a streaming mutual inflection. Eroding, permeating, attracting, harmonizing, perceiving, concentrating — all are instances of the flowing work of seams.

In constellations and seams we see that everything is multiple, and that everything flows. A flowing multiplicity of affects is an ATMOSPHERE.

> *Constellations and Seams: The Patina*
> *Should an antiquarian atmosphericist study the aged patina of a stout dining table from the countryside of France, she would see there the daily agglomerated residue of seaming constellations. Her practiced eye and hand would find, gathered atop and just into the wood's slightly absorbent surface, centuries of waxings rubbed up with dust and smokes, foods and finger oils, lints and inks, all cured by indirect sunlight and stratified in the varied layers of family fortunes. These constellated factors slowly seam together, thickening into the inimitable feel of a centuried patina held in the gravity of the table's bulky, dark form.*

The Seam Concept Refined:
The Cusps and Trailings of Seams

So far we have described the seam as if it were a simple and even occurrence, but in fact the seam is internally differentiated. For example, inside every seam are many cusps. The CUSP is an inmost edge of happening. It is a mutual threshold layer of intensified interchange where the seaming differential is most mercurial, sensitive, and ethereal. And then, too, seams can change over time, there being various stages of their action, from the brush of compressions before a seam's full engagement, to the affective lingerings of a seam's dissipation. The latter is called a TRAILING: the effusive wake of altering bodies. Technically, the antique patina described above — like all residues, memories, and aftermaths — is a trailing.

> *A Seaming Constellation with Cusps and Trailings: The Sound of a Note*
> *Each musical note is a seam gathering its specific constellation of anatomy, force, instrument, and style, and packing them into a single, if spiky, sonorous unfurling. The note's launch projects its pressures into the air, and through its flight the note decays, trailing along the still reverberating specificity of its manifold inception. This trailing is the note's sound over time. Across the note's entire trajectory there is a characteristic affect that variably flows on the very cusp of its mingling constellation precisely where the note sinks into scene and listener. This affect is* TIMBRE. *Not a disfigurement of the note's mathematical precision, but rather the very character of inclination that can be mathematically approximated, it is what we experience as a note: the signature irregularities of the blues' throaty voice in a smoky bar, the taut resonances of a quartet's fugue atop a polished*

wood stage, or the electronically antiseptic pulse of pop in the perfect clear space between headphones.

Every atmosphere, then, is populated by constellations riddled with flowing seams. The seams are fringed with cusps and waked by trailings.

2 | The Elements
AIRS, GRAVITIES, TIMES,
MINDS, LIGHTS, SOUNDS

Table 2.1

Sample Atmospheres

Element	Atmosphere 1	Atmosphere 2	Atmosphere 3	Atmosphere 4	Atmosphere 5
Airs	Ethereal and thin, this	Turbulent, the	Mellow and	Arid,	Coolish grit —
Gravities	collected substantial awe,	cutting levity,	sound,	effacingly buoyant,	compressed or eccentric or void
Times	all touchy and fleet,	punctuated and adverse,	simple provincial	and absorbed,	and weathered
Minds	acute,	gloomy,	copper	arcanely effusive,	nervy among
Lights	blue, opaque,	acrid	so sunny,	glimmers,	neon and dark, shiny
Sounds	prodigiously quavering	slander fast	hard, blunt	some giddy densities, prosaic reposes	bristlings

Airs

Loose gathering, the effusions, particulate of space, tumbling in whims of the midst, interspersed, aloft

Dankness and Cathedrals

There is a subtly tidal dankness that ebbs and flows in old cathedrals. The cathedral's rock-wall surfaces are pocked with millions of moist, microscopic dimples. And the surrounding air, relatively nimble and dry, happens across these porous surfaces, pulling with slow, randomized tenacity a cooling vapor from their minuscule, stony wells. This vapor gathers and flows first from the turreted apses where less air volume to wall surface results in higher humidity and fractionally more pressure. In these inverse chimneys, the air thickens with dankness most quickly, and then pours slowly downward, building, as it falls, a cumulating, humid momentum. Driven down by weight, coolness, and the light squeeze of air in the rigid tower, the dank creeps to the ground where, on impact, it tumbles in a slow-motion tumult and then flattens out across the floor. In a cathedral with apses at six points, four in the corners and two in the middle of the length of two opposing sides, the dank will pour down as described from each of the six points at a more or less equal rate to the floor where all six currents will meet and buckle upwards in one low, slow, fountainous splash in the center of the nave. When the cathedral's doors are closed for long periods of time, this contained fall-and-fountain cycle will pool cold, sober air up from the floor about the shins and pews and books. The rising and settling of bodies, and the turning of pages, churns the dank, blowing off feathery fragments that are occasionally inhaled and then murmured back out into the engulfing distances, generally gray and strewn with incense, chants, and the glint of chalices.

Cherry Blossoms

Coaxed by a celebrated, springtime seam of light, air, and maturation, cherry tree blossoms snap out in prolific clusters, white or pink, against barked wood. Unfurled into the aptly angled world, the blossoms seep their spores all strung with the oily strands of floral volatiles. When the day is still and cold, the scent is packed tightly in small volumes around each source-point blossom. When it is warm the scents dilate and merge about their tree into a single billowing redolence that in a breeze is drawn and thinned downwind, or in a gust tumultuously scattered. Delicate spawning playthings of hazard, these airborne baths hang and flow and happen onto bodies, inciting honeybees and office workers among the happenstance cloud forms and philosophies of nothing.

How Many Elements? Contemporary Debates

Some atmosphericists argue that the six atmospheric elements should be reduced to one at-bottom element, predicted but unobservable, that they call HAECCEITY. Others claim that there is no such fundament, but instead an infinitely proliferating number of elements that mingle throughout all dimensions in always singular ways. Ironically, both camps seek a one — for the reductionists it is the single one underlying all atmospheres that cannot be experienced in itself, whereas for the singularlists it is the innumerable single ones that permeate the particularity of every atmosphere and are necessarily experienced in themselves. This text works with the six elements, not as a compromise between the two but rather as a primer for the undecided, and to this end the reader might note instances of his or her own sense that there is something less below, or something more beyond.

Certain Doings of Dogs and Cats

The dog circles its chosen resting place to overwrite, with its own trailing scent, any lingering distractions of otherness. It thus creates in the air a circular atmospheric bridge of willfully solipsistic design — a temporary transition from wakeful wariness to slumbering, self-fulfilling security. While it's tempting to construe the zig-zagging walk of cats as a similar demonstration of their atmospheric hyper-sensitivity — a dodging and feinting about ambient rustlings — the zig-zags don't play around external impingements as much as they project from the cat's proclivities: the zig-zagging is a display of domesticated dexterity, the swagger of a predator curbed into the selected animal's jaunty, nimble, nervous dance.

Perfumed Skin

Consider first a honking city with its bordering river, outdoor cafés, flower stalls, steaming manhole covers, and blinking neon signs. Set within this hectic urban scene, a slender constellation of perfume and skin seems quite subtle, and not altogether heterogeneous — a slight, wispy accent of scent to scented body. But studied with finer-grained attention, the seam of perfume and skin reveals itself to be a very wide-ranging collection of constellated factors. This heterogeneity is particularly evident in the cusp of the perfume/skin seam, where atomized vaporlets are heated and shaken aloft into a blurry pointillist aerosol band suffused with salts and hormones, soaps and longings, foods and foments, all loosely held by the woolly thatch of a sweater, and warmed into an animal-citrus-allspice field of mooded happening. When the perfumed person walks, even in the scent-contested city, the flow of new air across their skin will pull the delicate cusp from its haven and leave a noticeable trailing: a swirling wake that faintly embosses the atmosphere with the ephemeral calling card of a passing physiology and taste.

Gravities

*Everything impinges — drawing tautnesses
in mutual earnest heaving holding situating
weightings — variously on everything*

Equitorial Lift

Flexing across the mass-spackled cosmos is a vast and invisible weave of mutual exertions that draw on the stars and planets, comets and dusts, passing photons and background x-rays (lingering cosmic birth cries of a non-point into everything). And we live within this weave, though here the straight-down attraction of our body to the Earth's center is the predominant force. And yet the massive spin of the planet — 1,000 mph at the equator fading at the poles toward zero — slightly dislocates this straight-down pull, bulging the Earth along the equator and flattening it at the poles, gripping the atmosphere at a sideways angle and mustering its densities into a play of whorls, jets, and fronts that pattern the planet as it rhythmically turns into and out of the sun. The spin's acceleration also affects smaller bodies, working a gentle vector of them: a super-subtle centripetal lift and thrust away from the surface that leavens things slightly more along the equator into the generally slow and buoyant clemency of the weather there. It is for this reason easier to walk eastward on the sultry equator with the planet's eastward roll than it is to walk in any direction near the cold, center-sunk disinclination of the poles.

Is There Quantity?
Contemporary Debates

One of the great ironies of atmospherics — a science that many consider to be a pure study of qualities — involves the question of quantity. Even if everything is mixed in everything, as Anaxagoras claimed, some believe that affects in a local atmosphere might be present in such small quantities that they are essentially (though never completely) without impact. Atmosphere thus potentially becomes a question of local concentrations: the quantity of a multiplicity. But others argue that quantities themselves — the pointed one, the lucky seven, the irrational ad infinitum — are qualitative abstractions of qualities. Thus, even some mathematicians can feel the dark oblong almost of the prime 19 the way someone with their eyes closed might feel an eggplant skin's midnight purples.

Momentum

Within the event there sometimes occurs some perfectly timed salience of aptitude — a definitive turn around which opens a slipstream of positive congruences. The way is eased for everything within that slipstream, but the slipstream is fringed with drag and cross-purposes, and for everything outside it the way is confounded. Following a turn in athletics, for example, momentum sweeps along the game's participants and constraints in two opposing directions, temporarily orienting happening into for- and-against. To achieve this bipolar heading across the field of play, momentum actually moves through all the grunting, blurry strains of action in a variety of directions and speeds, radiating from hips, heads, feet, and fingers, modulating itself intently all the way down into the turns of athletes in their media — into those seams where, for example, a hard-pivoting player twists his cleats' bite through soft turf, ripping the fine roots that sequentially hold and give beneath his flowing torque as he imparts impeccable touch to a ball. In athletics, as in desires, speeches, movements, and eras, MOMENTUM is the gravitational trailing of any real turn of the event.

Times
*Ongoing cadences in cadences,
cadences ongoing cadences*

Antique Clock Shop

The front door's jangle of bells opens into an intricately syncopated and widely distributed pattering — the ticks of hundreds of wound clocks filling a large store. Here one pumps its pistons atop a marble base, there another periodically launches an articulated cuckoo from behind a grained wooden door, and at the edges of the room the grandfather clocks stand watch, like coffins, with bloodless heartbeats and startling chimes. The clocks are sounding every second in their ticks of slightly different weights and timbres, some ticks longer and others shorter, many piling on one another or flowing out from one another, all bisecting the silence but never finally filling it. Every clock is paced by its metered expenditures of tension, and these expenditures work their way meticulously through the rhythmic idiosyncrasies of each mechanism: through the varied ores of their teeth, the varied tunes of their chimes, the varied conceptions of their motions. Both of a time and now in a time, and ever-so-slowly speeding up or slowing down, each clock clicks its interpretation of time out into the room, and the ensuing constrained commotion clatters about the keepers of the shop. Industriously pursuing their anachronistic occupation they have their eyes fixed all day on the turn of interlocking ratios, their ears drummed by the sonic thicket of ticks... Is it for them a maddening insistence of mortality, a near fullness of finitude, or just a mundane churn of mechanisms? As the keepers' moods and bodies change over the day and across the years, every clock, wound up to wind down, rolls its way along a much vaster flow from energy to entropy, and the shop is an articulate eddy of that flow, full of smaller and smaller eddies, all very calculatedly, very earnestly, unwinding.

Science or Meditation?
Contemporary Debates
There is a sentiment among some that atmospherics, with its penchant for infinitesimal findings gleaned at an untimely pace, is more a meditative practice than a rational undertaking. The progress-devoted mainstream of atmosphericists deny this vehemently. But they do quietly hope that the meditators might gain insight into the quiddity of atmosphere itself. For their part, the meditators hold that in light of the endlessly intricate patternings of atmosphere the meditative practice is the only sensible approach.

Beach Blur

Gravity swells out irregularly in the water, driving waves that beat the shore in sets before sinking back across the grainy sand. And the tide slowly stretches up onto land, or ebbs to the full depth of its own momentary complacency. Wind whips — local swaths of energy that burst and dash. Overhead, the steady, intense sun, unmoving, dazzles everything. Wave and tide and wind and sun: there is a soft, irregular collision of all these different rhythms on the beach that washes the particularities of time away. Time blurs and merges into a whole that is absorbed in all the vastness and moving energy, and so a huge span of day can happen without a distinguishing point. But then, when leaving, one slides into the warm silence of a car, and the gasketed thump of its shutting door sets the beach atmosphere apart. The engine revolves thousands of times per minute, the LCD clock glows green increments into the pleasantly tepid cabin, and beach time endures only in the sun-massaged thicknesses of muscles and the already contracting temperament.

Subway Cycles

Escalators cascade downward smoothly, their stepped belts sliding commuters to the long platforms and multi-car subway trains. Anticipations gather along all these lines and reach out through a tunnel toward the still imperceptible wind and whine of the train's weight. Its grinding mass enters the station over slatted rails, slowing along the platform as it bulldozes a building tangle of friction, heat, and noise up against the invisible limit of arrival. Punctually stopped on this limit, there is a caesura — the train admits a quick release of people into its compartments — and then, doors shut, it rebuilds momentum and speeds away. Time is like the escalator, or the tracks, or the train itself: a segmented line driving toward a specific point of arrival or departure. And yet all of these lines are imperceptibly curved: the escalator steps disappear into the ground before returning upward, the trains run on circuited tracks, and even the commuters rush toward some invisible destination only later to turn around and come back home. Most everything here is on a bigger or smaller cycle of time, and the station is a quotidian accelerator of these cycles, architected to expedite all the variously sized orbits that momentarily intersect within it. But spun or hidden from these march-step orbits, other temporalities are also at play. In the departed train's wake, for example, time slowly eddies on the platform, turning people around in the small distracted circles (briefest loopholes) now opened in their day. Momentarily off-kilter and relaxed, the people fold and refold newspaper stories, swipe screens, or unfurl meandering daydream threads that intersect with one another above the platform, sometimes exchanging tiny bits of narrative the way strands of DNA exchange bits of code. And here or there play out the cadences of blurry drunks, of riffing buskers, or of instant advertisements (those postered wormholes to sleeping pill silent moons or brisk mountaintop adventures) as the larger commute orbits fly insistently onward.

Museum Idiosyncrasies

A museum's floors, walls, and ceilings are usually pristinely smooth — cleansed of temporal calibration. Hung or sat on these abstracted surfaces the artworks keep their own idiosyncratic times. Here paints' viscosities were dripped down gestured gravities that stretch and blob or spatter a rhythmic punctuation of action and matter. On the polished floor smooth stones convert eons of tumble and erosion into a neatly piled enigma of contrivance. At the bottom of the stairs a glowing plasma quadrangle ripples with algorithmic irregularities. And off in a corner two big twists of welded metal brood slowly in the oxidizing afterglow of their violent creation. These works' varied times are poured out into the museum's architected spaces where they mingle with each other and with the flows of people down a spiraled ramp, across the vast, white-walled cubes of space, or in a quiet nook. Throughout these places the distinctive click of heels on hardwood floors ticks off different durations as people move through the seams of all these merging temporalities — the clicks might count out a wary dotted-line approach toward some giant, tempestuous presence across the room, or a close and lingering dance of angles about some persistently intricate fascination. And on a quiet weekday morning one might hear a guard's subtly modulating pace through the almost peopleless galleries.

The Beach City Estuary

In coastal cities beach time washes up into work time. It flows, for example, into the tall gray buildings where it is scooped by open elevators and lifted through their square shafts, poured across reception rooms and, more thinly, out toward the hallways and workspaces. A city like this is therefore an estuary of times, with the salty, mellow-stretched distraction of beach time periodically mingling with the cool productivity of conditioned time. On weekends the buildings, opened less frequently and left for the most part to themselves, become cold keepers of cubicled work, preserving the small efforts and strains of the previous week inside a correctly abstract time, neither engrossed by concentration nor blurred by the beach, but all slowly eaten at by the week's remnants of slightly salty air.

Sub-Discipline or Cosmology? Contemporary Debates
Some construe atmospherics as an inflection of existing areas of research. From their perspective, while both physicists and atmosphericists, for example, study time, sound, and color, the physicist abstracts from all these the quantities of periodicity, whereas the atmosphericist senses in them the affective idiosyncrasies of duration, timbre, and hue, respectively. Others ardently believe that atmospherics is instead a cosmology that considers all things to be variously viscous densities of atmosphere in flux. For these atmospheric cosmologists, wind is an unsettling; rock, a weighty recalcitrance; sunshine, a warm energy.

Minds
Perspicacious the involutions murmuring intensities, rustling, ramifying about

Library Concentrations

In places of silent, simultaneous intentness, as at a university library, calmed by summer, with few and slow motions, and people in various, limply rapt attitudes — pensive, querying, daydreaming, absorbed — there is a generative, hanging thickness about. Thoughts and thinkers have set up in a translucent slurry of engrossment that dampens down the place, draws minds out, and buffers concentration against smaller potential upsets. With focus recalibrated in the viscous stillness, even so-called distractions become zones of consistent attention: the concentrated mind moves adroitly, if gradually, suspended in this like-thickness, free to wield a finer attunement, running its slim hammer along a shelf's extensive xylophone of navy, olive, and burgundy cloth keys, softly sounding out the gilt-lettered tones of each binding with a small effusion of sense and spores. Or else gliding atop the smooth wood tables, retracing the swirls and stops of grain, growing self-absorbed in suggestive ink stains, or testing a gnarl's secretive grip about its distant reckoning of growth with climate. The clap of a reference work pancaking the floor (anticipated by a single, quiet gasp in the silence of the fall) will instantly harden and shatter the shared mental atmosphere. But most of what happens here is silently sunk within the thickness of concurrent concentration, a thickness subtly enriched by the sundry formulas and lists, diagrams and stanzas, syllogisms and speculations that slowly leach from the books into the broader, desklamp-lit solution. For unknown reasons, concentration in such a space is thinned when multiple minds consider a single topic.

Figments of Mind

There are allusive glimmers of thoughts — bare wisps or hoverings or inclinations of sense — each a local coalescence of affect, fleeting and lightly tinged with meaning. They flicker dimly like candles in the seams of memory, fantasy, and circumstance, wavering there among the shifting conditions of their own intensity, now gathering into something eminent, now extinguished in the rushing currents of happening. All of these mental, mooded, is but is-nots are FIGMENTS. One alone might dominate a moment of the mental atmosphere, while an entire phalanx of them might impart the barest of dispersing inflections, like a pinch of salt crystals ever more minutely quenched into a freshwater lake. A figment will rarely resolve. Sometimes this vagary persists because there is nothing other that it would resolve into: not short of a thought but sparsely flecked with it, it dangles in distantly intuited fields, nebulous in the characteristic bath of its own reflections. Other times the figment is so rarified that, even as it approaches a recognizable presence, it loses itself easily to its surroundings, like a skinless blimp aloft… The dream amorphosity is a figment that we fit, upon waking, with a succession of applicable but somehow always penultimate names, so that one was a tired cat or a footstool or lump or pillow, but it was always that irksome blobby softness on an otherwise empty floor. Grasped at words — words that we don't know if we are unsuccessfully recalling or intuitively inventing — are figments as well. These move along the different logics of the malaprop, pooling for example in the corner of a certain likely consonant and then running toward a family of significations. And the vague memory of an object suspected forgotten somewhere is a figment, too. This type generates a telling kite-tug from its presumed misplace, so that when we habitually leave things in haphazard places we are scattered: we leap and veer among the figments that condense first in a tray, then next to a bag, and then on a desk near a seemingly remembered thud of something dropped. Feeling along trains of recent events and frequencies of occurrence into drawers and closets and pockets, we are momentarily and uncertainly tethered to all those places, stuttering, sleuthing, plunging among the house-flung figments of a now pleated, tangled cusp of mind with time.

Food and Dreams

In the dark passages, the convolutions, musings, and salts, something is kept of the character of foods — kept and imparted to both the sleeper and his dreams. With some foods, the effort is immense, the successes periodic and significant, the effect on dreams more sporadic and pointed. In other cases, a steady spring is quietly offered up to dreams, thus left free to float and wander. Tubers, for example, impart a persistent drizzle of energy, rendering dreams dumb and enduring. Fish (particularly freshwater fish) dissolve neatly into soft, oily protein steams that smooth transitions along metaphoric turns of thought. The well-known violences produced in dreams from red meats devolve from the meats' specific densities. A cow must work cellulose cuds incessantly to build its stout yet toothsome sides of meat. And the flesh, tender but resilient, bears these accumulated churnings within churnings. When dislodged by a labored digestion, these churnings give way suddenly and thrash about in dreams of macabre moroseness, with car wrecks in filthy fields, with fearful stillnesses, detritus, and sweat, as the slow, mundane grazer disincarnates across osmotic gradients into vivid disturbances of mind.

Simpatico and Schooling Fish

There are fish that move as a school of thousands, all flashing in uniform vibrato before they twist as one around some abrupt cue and then pulse on. They swim in the fleet ambience of their correspondence, identically tuned to the smells, sights, and pressures that simultaneously ripple through their flexing bodies. And the school acts accordingly — as a single, circumspective organ of visceral simpatico, shuddering and shimmering its way through the signal-dense environs. SIMPATICO is not a reciprocated charisma of individuals, the schooling fish indicate, but instead a congruent resonance among them.

Mental Dawnings

On occasion, we register some indistinct and meddling bother, an increasingly urgent agitation on the back of our heads that finally compels us to whirl and look right into a set of eyes staring at us. Even across a large and crowded room we can somehow feel the irksomeness of the eyes on us, their vision boring its scrutiny into us. When a mental cusp is in this way ruffled by some immoderate protrusion of the environment, one senses an IMPENDING. So awkward jumps and flutters might smudge the cusp with the blurry-black syncopations of an injured bird, or a tiny alternating compression of air can be honed through the cusp into the pointed threat of a closing mosquito. From out of a distant and vague contiguity of the offing, something dawns on us — it touches us, and we realize it.

Is There Void or Is It a Plenum?
Contemporary Debates
Some argue that there can be no atmospheric void: the cosmos is a mottled plenum, and even the so-called void has an emptiness to it that is therefore affectively charged, if to a coldly blank extreme. Others believe that every atmosphere is actually riddled with void; that it is only with the spacing that void provides that seams can actually emerge and flow. For them, void flickers throughout matter along heterogeneous statistics of coming to be and passing away. The plenists elevate seams, encountering their flow literally everywhere, whereas the voidists emphasize constellations, presuming affectless gaps in happening.

Lights

Excited flights from encounters nimbly thatched at frequent angles and glancing passions' infinitesimal nuances across pliant fields

Iris Light

We peer into the world through the faintly tinted cones of light that are reflected forward from our own irises. The iris gathers the world's motley shine into its own hued and flecked, shallow bowl holding some frequencies within, casting some back, according to its color and to that of the lights that strike it. Within the forward shading that is cast by dark brown eyes, the brown iris comfortably drinks down even bright sunlight with hushed longing, the way churned earth absorbs steady rain. And this eye will field intensely saturated colors with a discrete yet concentrated ardency, as an otherwise featureless ground at night holds embers, lustrous against its dark, flat depths. In northern countries, where the airlight is often front- and back-scattered within the low ceiling of cloud cover, a bright gray glare bounds into and about a blue-gray iris with little inflection of its frequency, the eyes and sky encompassed in a resonant, lit-up light cycle of diffuse excitement. Green, gray, hazel, black irises — they all have their shifting affects in the shifting light. Light is, for us, precisely this variegated seam of mind and energy subtly inflected by the colored iris and flowing in the fastest possible tide of textures across our rod and cone feelers.

Shadows

Shadows cast a visual gravity that grounds things in light and fields. Shadows might, for example, connect saguaro to sun to desert in a seam where the cactus stands, starkly delineated, fearless of scorpions and unirked by vultures. Shadows also connect books to lamps on desks, raising the volume like a well-lit stage atop which plays the variously typed thoughts. And powerful stadium lights flow with the distant, barely shadowed actions of athletes about calibrated fields in the night. Without shadows, we would always be a little bit unmoored, as we are when floating lost in the diffuse and featureless fog, or during the unglued giddiness of dusk, when the just-set sun no longer grounds the hemisphere's more opaque bodies with the shape and depth defining blackish absences of light. Compare this buoyancy to the circumspectful awareness that surrounds a person walking beneath a number of strong, evenly distanced, overhead lights. He is connected to multiple sites on the ceiling and floor at once, and his shadow is correspondingly multiplied, with versions on one side lengthening and fading while those on the other contract and sharpen as the walker passes, like some smoothly manipulated marionette, beneath the downcast lines of light. We are, the shadows remind us, tethered to seams in the atmosphere, and, though moving about with relative freedom, doing so within the viscous constraints and emotive effluences of much that is both beyond us and yet pervading us. More specifically, the shadow carries an undercurrent of not being, projected only from those beings that actually are. It is for this reason that shadows are associated with the obscure, the occult, and the sinister. But these associations are limiting and exaggerated. For example, the sitting and promenading shadows of people in a sunny plaza currently offer little to fear, though, like all shadows, they do silently remind us that light shines on bodies in passing time.

Table 2.2

Night and Day

	Night	*Day*
Resolution	Obscure, enormous, the sparseness, with blackish pleatings around star-points, around each occasion,	Earth's arena is glared open minutely by infinite, star-printed swarms
Inflection	and everything drawn to slide away, sliding, breath to space, drawn by distant vacuums, the	come flight-aged through void to bounce and plunge here
Medium	air liquid, strewn with filmy moonlights, moths awash in it, intermittently inked in and out, and the jellies, thick, diaphanous, lax,	in wave-bath shimmerings, the widely disbursing band of light and its warmths
Action	riding prone, tentacles careless, tangling and untangling, caress of elongated rhythms, breathy cosines sinking out, some rambling about, some	touching off life to intent patterns of interplay
Exchange	distant, dimly streaking silence, sinking into the sparseness, sinking out	throughout the excited, scintillate sphere.

Television Light

Images fly invisibly from a television, casting as they travel a vague hue into the air. This is television light: a shapeless, bluish, programmed emanation that shifts speeds and densities according to the varied rhythms of genre and commercial interlude. Sitting before a television, and within this light, we fall under the sway of its dappled, flickering images, just as we are held by the play of a campfire. But with television, it is the fire itself telling the story, gesturing through an uncanny tint in the dark room that takes on the cast of an ersatz mental space where the lit perceptions of happening take priority, even as they mingle with the familiar, backdropped arrangements of our mentalities. In a room filled with daytime's brightness, some find television light's aura soothing, and they might nap with the television on and muted, their biorhythms lightly swayed by its electromagnetic waves, their dreams jumping in some heady world mostly hidden from the washed-out gleam that still plays across the dreamer's face. Elsewhere, as in the corner of a restaurant's bar, a television reaches out indifferently from its perch like an oblivious drunk talking to no one in particular. Television light feels lonely, its endlessly eager dance caring so much and at the same time so little for our desire. That desire sated, touch a button and the specter instantly retracts into its circuitry, trailing but an instant's blasé afterglow.

Sounds
Timed textures of pressure, expressively palpating their frictioned sources along mediated flights

The *Patio Escondido* and Its Fountains

Some houses in southern Spain have a courtyard that is heat-sheltered between the walls of their U-shaped architecture. Even from the street one can occasionally glimpse through the black iron twists of a gate an aisle or corner of this lush domestic labyrinth, with heavily watered plants and an empty, half-forgotten pot, some tiles propped up against a wall, and perhaps a fraction of a window and its sill, dotted with intense red bulges of geraniums (like elaborate blood organs, turned inside out, unwavering in the heat). Through the gate seeps a moist, organic oxygen of wet plants, clay, and stone, its gauzy vapor invisibly sewn with the cadenced, cosine plashings of a fountain. Some fountains' deep, slow, periodic plunks invoke an amniotic reminiscence, sending single soothing liquid beats into the patio's shades and recesses, and out to its insulated walls. Other fountains cascade cheerfully, the water's falling surges, tributaries, and mists cooling the air close to the fountain while its playing sounds lift the patio's uncertain moods.

Sonic City Jumble

Cities generate irregular sonic cacophonies. Screeches and honks, rumbles and shouts, clicks, taps, and talk, barking, scrapes of all sorts, vendor hawking, and machinic grindings — all these bounce and clash and surge about the pavement and walls, the moving cars, the curbs, and foyers of the city. The jumble of differently timed energies bangs and slops about, only here and there finding some stride among the blink of stoplights and within the broader rhythms of commerce and pleasure, season and culture. Across these strands of order the differently timed energies drive at awkward angles through the city: the crash of an aluminum trashcan will shoot powerfully from an alley like a bullet from a rifle, or the rattling slide and bang of a truck's cargo door will repercuss off a nearby glass-slabbed skyscraper. But enter the atmospheric pocket of a well-insulated building — say a peaceful Japanese tea room, all deep silent cement surfaced with whispering textures — and you feel the contrastive quiet shielded from the city's sonic slosh. Behind you the door shuts — the rustling black bristles along its bottom sweeping back the noise, even as its arcing plane draws a little of the lingering sound back into the room, generating as it swings through the quiet a last, small cyclone of city noise, a beep-barking filigree that spins up and plays itself out quickly, disbanding in the cooler air and dispersed street dust at the now-closed entrance. The resealed room is again left completely to its restrained and delineated sounds as single strings are plucked from recessed speakers, and thick ceramic cups thud on wood.

Ambient Music

Music is an undulant — its articulate waves modulate and tinge the ambience. They pulse its volumes rhythmically, seeking its reaches to the fading limits of their energy, and their sonic-friction loss in flight is a subtle gain in air and light and thought according to each element's capacity to absorb the colored, cadenced compressions of time. Indoors, ambient music discreetly propagates its mooded shapes throughout the room, pervasive, yet backdropped, like an invisibly dimensionalized wallpaper. Hard surfaces reflect and angle music, whereas fuzzy textures snag it, the waves gently losing themselves, for example, in a deep rug oblivion with but a dusty, microscopic rustling of woolen fibers. Indoor air particles, jostled and buffed by music's winds, are slightly freshened. And plants — gentle, rooted plyers of the ambience — are pervious to its undulations, generally flourishing among the micro-ordered waves of sound. The plant's broad diurnal rhythms are freshly patterned by music with relatively minute and rapid proportions — time, in other words, is structured, sped and mooded around the plant, and the plant climbs the fleeting lattices of sound even as it gainfully absorbs their stimulating modulations.

3 | Applications
Studies prominently involving multiple elements

Camouflage
Lights, Times, Minds

Everywhere the surroundings sink through everything differently (picture refraction, consider acculturation). The camouflaged animal can channel the surroundings through its densities, its proclivities, and its motions into a self-effacing gesture of its niche, but not without absorbing the implications of its guise. Take the octopus — as it floats with its vagrant intelligence through diverse haunts, it assumes the changing senses of the ambience in its body. But before it slips fully into camouflage it sometimes shows an incongruous, rippling-colors delay. Once regarded as a visible run-through of the possibilities being queried from the creature's spectral well, these colors are now seen as an expression of the creature's moods leaking through its camouflage as it feels itself adopting a new surrounding. Camouflage is a thorough interchange, not a surface mimicry, and in this interchange, as the surroundings sink through the mercurial and impressionable octopus, they might incite a moment's emotion, but they might also expand the palette of moods that the octopus can feel and exude back into the varying waters.

The Produce Aisle
Lights, Airs, Times, Minds

In the cool of a grocery store's produce section, with its staid, evenly lit displays, the colors of the fruits project the farthest. Stacked in sections along the aisle, they emit the color-coded bands of their specific atmospheres. On a certain day, the eye might take in green hippy pears, bending yellow banana bunches, and tan cratered cantaloupes (uncanny as the plucked moons of some distant, oft-pelted planet). With color as wayfinder, one can move more definitively into specific segments of the aisle's spectrum. Now, projecting from the fruit type and shape, are the details of blush and bruises, textures and mottlings — details all sharpened in each fruit's near-field effusion of scent. Picked up, and assayed in the lift and drop of a hand, the fruit's density moves suggestions through fine to gross musculature and back into shifting dispositions of desire and expectation. A tiny violence to the fruit releases more sense for consistency, juice, and flavor: a thumb-tip, for example, shallowly dimpled into an apple, practices either a satisfied crunching bite or a mealy disappointment. Or the pluck of a pineapple's leaf lets the ooze of its sharp perfume into the air, across needled taste buds and squeezing salivary glands. Even encased in its gold and brown, sugar-bruised armor, we thus already sense the pineapple's unique intensity of tropical reproductive intention, the stinging rush of this sweet liquid fiber acid sun, inwardly fissioning fructose and vitamin C next to complacent, green grapes in the tidy store.

Pluralist Symphony
Sounds, Times, Minds, Gravities, Lights

People will sit about a symphony hall, arranged in plush seats, listening to the rampant-nervous shriekings of a musical crescendo. The sound, let rambunctiously from strings and hollows, lips and valves, storms about the room, slamming against acoustic surfaces, crashing toward the red-stenciled exits, frothing headspaces, and threatening to rip bodies free from chairs like kites in a tempest. The thrashing energy is splintered everywhere in the sonic torrents: even along the neck of a single violin with its four strings the sounds are multiply built and multiply sent, multiply deflected and multiply returned. And through the commotion the images of the various players — bowing, pounding, rocking — fly ahead of the sounds that their motions produce, with the stretch of image from sound lengthening as the emanations reach further from the stage. The music drives conflicting momentums that surge around the people, agitating their anticipations and consternations, stirring their anxieties and deliriums. Many of the people vibrate with a sense of unfulfilled cataclysm, yet outwardly there is little shown for it among the staid, seated bodies beyond some small ventings in scattered coughs, or the occasional shift of posture, or a single fiery glare that shines a tiny fraction of the energy back into its rampantly fraying sources.

Terroir
Airs, Times, Lights, Gravities, Minds

A vine's roots grapple with the singularities of its earth — the densities, the elements and minerals, the drainage. And its woody stem contorts helically aloft, spreading trained, gnarled, sinewy arms out into the clime to be aired and sunned, dampened with fog, compressed by cold, relaxed by heat. Within these arms, the genetically inclined bunches are raised on the timed angles of daylight and winds, of economic yields, human palates, and seasonal rains, all flowing across and through the increasingly particularized grapes. After being picked, crushed, and metabolized by yeasts, a liquid is drawn from the grapes — a liquid raw in its reminiscence, ripe with its own let vitality — and poured into a single-chambered, oaken barrel, its walls a stiff, dry membrane. Ambient airs seep slowly inward across this membrane, drawing as they go the toasted wood's coaxed redolences of tobacco, vanilla, and tea. And across the barrel's inner surface, from each of its innumerable pores, open plumes of air into the dense scarlet morass — deeply scented plumes that diffuse with difficulty, drifting slowly inward. The wine respires this way for some months. Then it is drawn, apportioned, and confined for years within its non-reactive glass bottle, left to meditate there on its own still and viscous thisness. When the bottle is opened, the wine released into its glass is a dark liquid star, heavy and smoldering coolly beneath its swirling vapors. It only slowly involves itself in the startlingly alien atmosphere, drawing in the air, and effusing its own qualities just beyond the top of its glass and into the room's night. Through it all, and even across the palate and into the bloodstream, the wine bears its native genes, minerals, and clouds.

Current Trends in Atmospherics

Though instrumentation remains crude, and computing power inadequate, leaps in thought have the field of atmospherics in a vital state. A handful of representative topics are described below.

Molecular Memory
Advances in theory have led to the discovery of variation among molecules in an absolutely pure, evenly heated, and pressured volume of water. Efforts to trace these persistent differences back to structural variations in the molecules have proven fruitless. It is currently hypothesized instead that water molecules — and, by extension, all molecules — carry forward the still affective vectors of their pasts as an expressive way of going (a non-random Lucretian swerve) that is unrelated to structure. Studies of water volumes, translated into 3-dimenionsally imaged data fields, reveal a box of fuzzy cloud forms continuously sliding around one another. When color is added to indicate affect, one sees a shifting, chromatic mélange of picometric clouds, with an individual's hue altering (according to projections) on a timeline of decades, while its specific shade responds immediately if just slightly to the molecules that brush past it.

Climate Change
The ambience of climate change is a vast and daunting prospect for atmosphericists to assay, though breakthroughs have been made by certain researchers with expertise in medieval apocalyptics, and, from a completely different angle, in kitsch art. Early results indicate that the time-honored convergence of complexity and uncertainty, with all its various pockets and fissures of difference, does seem to be broadly acquiring a foreboding cast.

Would We Tune the Waves?
Contemporary Debates

The recent rise in data-rich waveforms that now permeate our atmosphere is clearly having some effect, and this has become a subject of fierce debate. There are some who claim that if we are to be barraged, we ought to tune the inundation. Randomization affords better protection against coercion, but orchestration, the other side avers, could bring us echoes of the ancients' well-tuned spheres.

Atmospheric Viscosity
The atmosphere is loaded with forces that variably alter its thickness and give. On Earth our air-vapor, the vectors of gravity, the warbling white shafts of starlight, propagating bosons — all this and more merges into a viscosity of the atmosphere that is largely unperceivable but affectively present to things as a fluctuating bath of weights, speeds, and frictions. Over time, atmospheres' viscosities change, and historical data gained from tiny samples captured in blown glass are now being plotted against large events in cultural histories (revolutions, dark and golden ages, emergent economic orders, etc.) in an ambitious attempt to determine the influence of cultural events on atmospheric viscosity, and, in turn, of atmospheric viscosity on cultural events.

Seams and Perception
The more broadly scaled work on atmospheric viscosity was in fact spurred some years ago by prior research into perception. We produce an envelope of receptivity that enmeshes itself, and us with it, into the atmosphere. Perception too, in other words, is a complex seam, and though the perceptual response to an environment has been studied since antiquity, we have only in the last decades begun to consider how the playing, viscous envelope of perception actually affects the atmosphere within which it is enmeshed. Research in the studios of painters who depict still-life arrangements have yielded interesting results on this topic, particularly as the paintings themselves capture elements of the atmosphere that can be used to corroborate the researcher's findings, though one always needs to correct for the noxious impacts of the different paints.

quale [kwa-lay]; *Eng.* n 1. A property (such as hardness) considered apart from things that have that property. 2. A property that is experienced as distinct from any source it may have in a physical object. *Ital.* pron.a. 1. Which, what. 2. Who. 3. Some. 4. As, just as.

www.ingramcontent.com/pod-product-compliance
Lightning Source LLC
Chambersburg PA
CBHW031208090426
42736CB00009B/837